The Colosseum

A Captivating Guide to an Icon of Ancient Rome Known for Hosting Roman Gladiator Battles and Public Spectacles

Free Bonus from Captivating History (Available for a Limited time)

Hi History Lovers!

Now you have a chance to join our exclusive history list so you can get your first history ebook for free as well as discounts and a potential to get more history books for free!

Simply visit the link below to join.

Or, Scan the QR code!

captivatinghistory.com/ebook

Also, make sure to follow us on Facebook, X, and YouTube by searching for Captivating History.

Table of Contents

Introduction

The Colosseum is one of the most easily recognized structures from ancient times (along with the Great Wall, the Parthenon, and Stonehenge), but there is a lot more to the famous ruins than most people realize. While there are a lot of movies and media that cover gladiator tournaments, these were only a part of the Colosseum's history. So much happened within those iconic, round walls that are both entertaining and horrifying, especially as Rome played such a vital role in the history of an entire continent.

From its inception, the Colosseum has been a symbol, although the meaning of the structure has changed over the millennia. Emperor Vespasian had his own plans for the grand structure when he initiated its construction sometime between 70 and 72 CE. It took roughly a decade to complete the massive arena, and it was one of the tallest structures in Europe for centuries. Able to hold up to possibly eighty thousand people, the Colosseum became one of the best places to visit in Rome.

Emperor Titus had come to power by the time the Colosseum was completed, and he ensured that the newly constructed facility was something people would be discussing for a long time, though he likely had no idea that people would still be aware of it over two millennia later. Almost as soon as the structure was completed, it had a one-hundred-day celebration of gladiatorial games. When the throngs of celebrators arrived, they were greeted by an impressive, three-story structure that has withstood the ravages of time, wars, and disasters, representing Rome long after the empire fell. Even today, it remains an incredibly impressive structure, but it must have been a truly impressive structure when it was first built.

Over time, the Colosseum moved from being a place of entertainment to a place used by the emerging Roman Catholic Church. It was a fortress during medieval wars and became a dilapidated structure when the elements and the sands of time began to break away parts of the structure. Earthquakes and human warfare were far more damaging than vandalism, but pollution caused the worst damage to the structure, as it eroded the walls and lower levels.

As it lost its relevance as a place for entertainment and became too dangerous for casual use, people and communities in the surrounding areas began to pull out all of the valuable components, including marble and ivory, from the once magnificent structure. For roughly one thousand years, this symbol of a lost empire was seen as a quarry to be used to build up growing towns and cities around Italy.

The historical importance of the structure wasn't considered until the 1800s, and it was then that efforts were made to preserve it. While it had lost a lot of its opulent components, the Colosseum is still a spectacular ruin that shows just how capable the Romans were at creating buildings and other structures. It has become one of the biggest attractions; people from all over the world visit this historical marvel for themselves to experience a fraction of the splendor that Romans experienced over two thousand years ago.

Chapter 1 – Planning and Construction

Well over 1,500 years since Rome ceased to be an empire, we still use the expression "Rome was not built in a day," indicating just how impressive the empire once was. It actually took the Romans several hundred years to create the structures, government, and culture that lived on long after their civilization had collapsed.

Part of what helped to shape the empire was the way the Romans took inspiration from their neighbors, even though they fought those same neighbors. The ties that the Romans had with Greece were obvious in many aspects of their burgeoning culture, especially in their religion. The Romans had the same gods and goddesses as the Greeks but gave them different names and personalities. Over time, the traits of the Roman pantheon adapted to take on the values of the Romans. In the same way, Greek architecture influenced early Roman works, which is clear from the way the Colosseum appears, as it looks similar to Greek architecture. However, they weren't the only neighbors the Romans took ideas from. The Etruscans were another notable civilization that influenced Roman culture and architecture. Rome was one of the most dominant powers in North Africa and Europe for hundreds of years. However, the empire had its fair share of poor rulers. Emperor Nero was so awful that his name remains synonymous with horrible, callous rulers over two thousand years later. Emperor Nero lost the ruling family a lot of support from a large portion of the Romans who could actually force change.

Nero's inability to rule is unknown. Some historians have attributed his horrible methods of ruling to a range of issues, such as mental health and genetics. Other historians have attributed his failed tenure as emperor to the very things that people have been saying since Nero's death, saying he was selfish and that his actions were a reflection of more modern diagnoses, such as psychopathy and a lack of concern for the people under his care.

Emperor Vespasian, who was the emperor who ruled after the succession crisis after the death of the incompetent Nero, knew that it would be important to regain the people's trust. After all, there had been a string of rulers in quick succession. Rebellions and changing alliances were typical of this period, which was called the Year of the Four Emperors. It is thought that the Colosseum was a calculated move to gain the respect of the population who were turning against the rule of an individual. Emperors who understood the importance of winning over the people often started with a populist movement in the beginning. Vespasian hoped not only to show off how strong and capable the Romans were but also to rebuild trust and favor after several disastrous emperors. Vespasian wanted to show the people that he was the kind of ruler who would focus on improving the empire, offering the kinds of entertainment and pride that had once helped the people celebrate the strength of Rome. To do this, he needed to help them forget his predecessors. The Colosseum was a new kind of solution, as there wasn't anything quite like it.

Since Emperor Vespasian had been the one to emerge victorious after the succession crisis, there was still the question of whether his reign was legitimate. He was well aware of how important it was to ensure that he was able to quickly get as many people on his side as possible.

While not the most effective Roman ruler, Emperor Vespasian did have a good understanding of how to win over the people. In an effort to help remove Nero's memory, the Colosseum was built in the location that Nero had owned, where he had kept a garden around a lake. Part of Emperor Vespasian's plan to regain popularity was to dedicate lands associated with Nero's excesses to the people. He wanted to turn those areas into places to celebrate Rome so they would no longer represent the pampered life of a few elites.

Since the plan was to build an enormous theater for sports, the lake, which had been a favorite spot for Nero, had to be drained. This served the dual purpose of clearing the area for a large amphitheater and removing the potential risks that a lake posed in an area where earthquakes remained a threat to the people living in the region. Another measure implemented at the beginning of the Colosseum's construction (specifically to counter the threats posed by earthquakes) was to add concrete foundations that went down six meters, or nearly twenty feet.

Ironically, Nero theoretically allowed everyone access to his lands, but it upset the Roman senators since they didn't think that common people should be allowed to visit locations that they thought should only be used by the elite. Emperor Vespasian was removing a "special place" for the few people who considered themselves above everyone else, and he really couldn't afford to go entirely against them. The structure offered a unique compromise. Nearly anyone would be allowed into the Colosseum, but the more prominent and "important" Romans would be allowed to have areas that were inaccessible to the masses.

Even though Emperor Vespasian was no longer in power when the Colosseum was finished, his descendants kept the same plan, establishing areas where only people who were considered the most important could go. The elite would have places of prominence so they could watch from the best locations. They would also be visible to the masses.

The different seating areas were identified as follows:

- The podium was for the elite members of the Roman Empire.

- The gradation was the seating for important people who had served but had not reached the highest echelons of power.

- The porticus was for the masses, and while it wasn't as comfortable as the other two areas, the people were still able to enjoy the same events. It was far more inclusive than what most other emperors had given them.

The rows closest to the activities belonged to the emperor, his family, and the members of the Senate. The next few rows belonged to those who were a part of the equestrian order (veterans of the Roman cavalry), merchants, bureaucrats, and artisans—people who had managed to earn positions where they would be recognized for their skills. The rest of the seats belonged to the common people, who made up the majority of the Roman Empire. This is actually the way many stadiums are structured today, with the best and most comfortable seats being reserved for people who are considered important (although these people tend to also include relatives to those playing the sport), and the seats higher up are for everyone else. For example, at a basketball game, floor seats would be reserved for important people, and at concerts, the first few rows are often reserved for family, friends, contest winners, and other people who are "important" for some reason.

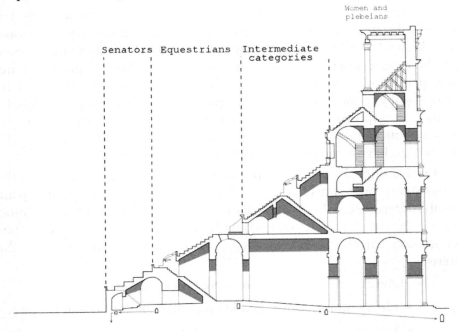

The seating of the Colosseum.[1]

During the design process and construction, the architects provided four entrances exclusively for the important people, who made up roughly 5 percent of the population. For the other 95 percent of people coming to watch the games, there were seventy-six entrances. Separate corridors were made to ensure that the people who were considered important were able to move through the halls without having to mingle with everyone else.

Once people were in their seats, they were largely able to get the same view as everyone else. Obviously, the farther a person was from the action, the less they were able to see, but they weren't entirely excluded from enjoying the games.

Other similar structures of that time were temporary. The Colosseum was unique because it was constructed with a long-lasting material: concrete. The use of this more permanent material has allowed the Colosseum to remain over two thousand years after the people who built it died. It is impressive because the area where it was built was considered a wetland. Even though flooding and poor soil hindered building, the Romans ensured a much more stable structure by digging deep into the dirt, giving it a solid foundation. Concrete was not the only material, though, as it was mixed with travertine stone and bricks.

It included some impressive inner workings as well, things that are not done today. For example, the Romans had a very robust irrigation system that helped them to better tend to farming. They used similar construction methods for the Colosseum, creating a drainage system that allowed them to fill the arena so they could recreate sea battles for people to watch. The builders installed an awning, and the Romans hired sailors who extended and retracted the awning during the rain and heat.

However, perhaps the most impressive part is still visible today: the network of tunnels and chambers under the arena, which was called the hypogeum. An intricate system of gears and levers allowed for people, animals, and props to be lifted into the arena instead of having to walk out onto the field. This made for much more dramatic entrances for battles, plays, and spectacles. The largest participants brought to the arena in this way were elephants, demonstrating that the Romans were able to make devices that were capable of impressive feats.

Because of the turmoil that the Roman Empire was in at the time of Emperor Vespasian's reign, the financial records for this period are unknown. However, there has been speculation that the Romans were able to fund this impressive architectural feat by sacking the Temple of Jerusalem. This ensured that the Roman people didn't feel that their money was being wasted on an awe-inspiring attraction. This would have been an incredibly effective way of showing Roman strength. They could take from the people under their control to celebrate themselves.

As mentioned, Emperor Vespasian started the project around 72 CE, but he did not live long enough to see it completed. His son, Titus, took power following Emperor Vespasian's death, so when the Colosseum was unveiled in 80 CE, he was the one to gain the benefit from it. When it was opened that year, he decreed that there would be one hundred days of games, ensuring that people from far and wide would be able to attend. This provided a distraction to the problems that were plaguing the empire, and the people thoroughly enjoyed the spectacles.

A coin from Titus's reign celebrating the opening of the Colosseum.[2]

However, the Colosseum wasn't actually completed until 83 CE, by which time Titus had died, and his brother, Domitian, was in power.

Many of the workers on the Colosseum were Jewish slaves brought in after Rome sacked Jerusalem. They not only provided the labor but also a lot of the funding for the impressive structure. The number of estimated slaves used varies, but most agree that it would have required several thousand slaves from start to finish.

When it was finished, the Colosseum was 6 acres inside, with the surrounding entryways creating a circumference of 545 meters. For a long time, it was one of the tallest structures in the world, reaching 48 meters (157.5 feet), which is roughly the height of a 12-story building today.

Chapter 2 – Original Appearance and Early Renovations

Even today, the appearance of the Colosseum is iconic, and it is still easily recognized by people from around the world, despite it being a ruin of its original design.

A view of the Colosseum.[3]

There are many mysteries associated with the structure. The first one goes back to the very core of the Colosseum. The person or people who designed the structure are entirely unknown today. Concrete was used for a lot of the critical components of the Colosseum because its architects understood how strong it was. The Romans had been using the material for some time, but the Colosseum was one of the largest and most extensive uses of concrete in a single structure. The fact that concrete was at the literal foundation of the Colosseum is why it has been able to withstand natural disasters and countless wars.

One of the most noticeable features of the Colosseum is its great height. Four floors surrounded the arena when it was first built. Both the second and third floors were adorned with enormous statues. Although it does look like a circle from some angles, once inside, it is clear that the shape is elliptical to allow for a larger audience. Even today, there are impressive arches that circle three of the four rows. The arches are actually what made the structure so sturdy. Architects used arches because they allowed for substantial weight to be evenly distributed. By using this particular architectural staple, they were able to create buildings that have been able to withstand the test of time. The statues made the building look more regal.

The original Colosseum had brick around the exterior. People plundered different parts of the structure over the years, leaving less than half of the original brick on the structure by the Middle Ages. The interior had marble and other precious resources that were removed over time, so very little of the original opulence has been left. The concrete withstood the thefts because it could not be easily removed, and it is now the most notable material that remains of the impressive structure.

The exterior and the foundation were concrete throughout the arena, but most of the seats were made of stone. The wealthier individuals would bring cushions to sit on. The seats were inclined in a way that is similar to stadiums today, allowing people better visibility, no matter where they were seated.

Not all of the changes made to the Colosseum after its initial construction related to improving the structure. A lot of the later construction work focused on repairs and maintenance, even when it was still fairly young.

Based on more recent understandings of the structure, some of the corridors were painted or covered in colored plaster. It is thought that the colors were black, green, red, and yellow. It is known that there was a devastating fire at the Colosseum in 217 CE, and some archaeologists hypothesize that the original four colors were destroyed in the fire. Instead of spending the time and money to restore the corridors to their original appearance, the Romans opted for a much simpler red and white. The Roman Empire was in decline by this time, so it was likely necessary to be more economical.

The structure was struck by lightning during the 3rd century, causing further fire damage. While repairs were made, it was done at a much slower rate, taking a couple of decades to complete. The repairs were not nearly as thorough or detailed as previous repairs.

The last known time that the Romans worked to repair the structure was around 443 CE. That year, Rome experienced a significant earthquake, resulting in the top tier of seats being almost completely destroyed. By this time, the use for the structure had been altered, as it no longer held gladiator contests, so the Romans did not have nearly as much concern for maintaining the Colosseum. While they did some work, it was not detailed and was much more haphazard than previous restoration and maintenance work. They did not even bother completing the repairs. Less than one hundred years later, the Colosseum saw its last major event, and it soon became repurposed once Rome ceased to rule Europe.

Much of the beauty of the Colosseum that was enjoyed by the Romans is long lost to time. The opulence of what it once was has been lost to the weather, fire, and plundering. It is impossible to know everything that was used or exactly how it looked since most of the important materials have been removed, except for the impressive shell. Even so, the Colosseum remains an incredible piece of history that continues to show that ancient Rome was capable of creating marvelous structures, some of which are possibly even more stable and resilient than any structure being made today.

Chapter 3 – Naming the Architectural Wonder

Although the massive structure has come to be known as the Colosseum, it has had many names since it was first constructed. Originally, it was called the Flavian Amphitheater, although it would have been known as Amphitheatrum Flavium at the time. There is nothing subtle about the name. The title bears the name of the family that commissioned and presented the structure to Rome, the Flavian dynasty, giving them credit for building such an impressive structure. The other part of the name is entirely unimaginative as it simply describes what the structure is—an amphitheater. While histories and history buffs likely know the original name, most people are almost completely unaware of the Flavian dynasty and its role in creating the amazing structure.

At a glance, it is easy to imagine that the name comes from the sheer size of the structure. Perhaps this is one of the easiest ways to remember the name when first learning about it, but that is not where the name derives from.

Ironically, the structure has come to be known by a name that is also attached to Emperor Nero. Since Emperor Vespasian was working to replace the areas associated with his predecessor, one of the things that was located near the place where the Colosseum was to be built was a thirty-meter (nearly one-hundred-foot) statue of the late emperor. The statue was called the Colossus of Nero, and it was considered one of the greatest wonders of the world at that time. The statue was impressive, making it a fairly good complement to the enormous structure. This is an example of how Emperor Vespasian and other rulers of the Flavian dynasty were different from Nero since they made things for everyone to enjoy instead of creating massive to celebrate himself. However, as time progressed and the events of Nero's reign and the tumultuous year of the Four Emperors became something largely lost to time, people failed to realize that the name of the statue was transferred over to the structure, which was meant to be the antithesis of that very statue.

While there were a lot of negative associations with Nero, his statue was still viewed as a wonder and demonstrated the ingenuity of Rome. The people were proud of it. It has been said that Saint Bede the Venerable once wrote, "As long as the Colosseum exists, Rome will exist; when the Colosseum falls, Rome will fall also; but when Rome falls, the world will fall too." He was a monk during the Middle Ages, showing that both the Colosseum and the Colossus were still around or were at least well known around the world (Bede never went to Rome to see either structure).

It seems unlikely that Bede wrote this, but someone from his time period did, so the quote has often been misattributed to him. Some have thought that this writer was talking about the Colosseum, but it is much more likely that he was talking about the statue of Nero. At the time, the structure was probably still known as the Flavian Amphitheater. The writer specifically mentioned the Colyseus, which is generally considered a reference to the statue. As a scholar who was writing around the 7th century, he was more likely to know which of the two structures was at greater risk because the weather and the tectonic plates could do more damage to a single statue than to an entire structure. Also, by that time, Roman power and influence were not what they once had been.

The statue had been repurposed over the years, with people saying that it was Apollo, not Nero, by the time the Colosseum opened. When Emperor Hadrian was in power, it was said that it represented him; the famous wall that he built in modern-day northern England is what this emperor is most remembered for today. Toward the end of the Roman Empire, the people once again decided that it was a representation of Apollo instead of a specific emperor.

The fact that the statue was the focus of so much attention and change indicates that it was an important symbol to Rome. While the purpose of the Colosseum changed over time, its purpose was entertainment, at least while Rome was still an empire. It had a purpose beyond being impressive; the statue was merely a symbol. This is why it is thought that Bede or whoever wrote that passage was referring to the statue, not the structure.

And this author proved to be right. Unlike the Colosseum, the Colossus of Nero did not withstand the test of time. Today, the only remaining part of the once-impressive piece of art is the pedestal on which the statue stood. The statue fell, as did the power of the Roman Empire. However, the Colosseum did not.

By 1000 CE, it seemed as if the Colosseum was no longer being celebrated as an architectural marvel. It seemed that many of the symbols of Roman ingenuity were disappearing. The first time that the term "Colosseum" was used to reference the amphitheater was around 1061 CE when it was documented in the archive of Santa Maria Nova (today known as Santa Francesca Romana, a Catholic church in Rome). In this writing, the structure was referred to as Amphitheatrum Colossei. From there, it began being discussed in other writings, particularly by pilgrims to the region. During this time, the structure came to be known as the Colosseum.

Today, the structure is called the Colosseum, but when spelled out, it is both the Colosseum and the Coliseum. For the most part, the terms are used interchangeably because using either term brings to mind the right structure. However, it has been argued that "Colosseum" is the correct name when talking specifically about the Roman amphitheater, with the "C" being a capital letter.

Chapter 4 –The Arena and Amenities

Today, people often think that the Colosseum was a place for the gladiators and a few theatrics. The structure housed so much more than that. It was a place of games and spectacles that we don't have today. Movies and shows allow us to get a glimpse of that kind of entertainment, though. We don't have any comparable structures today because there is no place to go to witness water battles on that scale in an enclosed arena. You either have to watch them on the actual water or on a screen.

When it was fully completed, between fifty thousand and eighty thousand people could come and watch events and celebrations. Conceived as a way to remind Europe of the might of Rome, the Colosseum was the most complex building of its time and would remain the most complex building for over a millennia. To this day, it is still the largest amphitheater humans have ever completed.

As mentioned in Chapter 2, a lot of considerations went into the design so that the Romans would have the ability to really impress the people who came to the events. The place that remains perhaps the most inspiring is the hypogeum, the area under the Colosseum.

The Arena

Most of us have seen movies or shows that depict what the arena looked like when it was used for spectacles. Actually seeing the structure in person creates an entirely different feeling because it feels so much more real. You can more easily imagine what it was like to attend a game in person back in ancient times. It is somewhat similar to watching a football game versus actually attending one. While you won't be able to watch any games today, you can tour the engineering marvel in a way that was not available to most people who lived in ancient Rome.

Looking at the grounds, the place looks very open. Visitors are able to see the stones that held up the arena and the labyrinthian area under the structure. The arena itself largely isn't there now because it was not made of earth. The mechanisms and other moving parts under the structure would not have worked, nor would they have been able to have the stunning water battle reenactments, if they had been under actual ground. Since the Romans built over a drained artificial lake, the area was already open.

When the Romans began having gladiator fights and other spectacles, they placed wood panels over the underground area. This hid what was happening from the spectators. Once the panels were placed, staff would add layers of sand over them to create a more natural look to the fights. The sand was collected and brought from Monte Mario, a hill in the northwestern part of Rome, which was a fairly short distance from the Colosseum. Still, it was an impressive feat, as they needed enough sand to cover 83 meters by 48 meters (272.3 feet by 157.5 feet). When the panels were placed, they were set up so that animals, people, and props could be brought up through the floor instead of being walked out onto the grounds.

The seating closest to the arena was not on the same level because it could have put the very important spectators at risk. The stands were raised up roughly 3 to 4.5 meters (10 to 15 feet) from the arena, creating a large wall that would be nearly impossible to scale and providing protection from whatever was happening.

Where much of the Colosseum is white or cream colored, the wall around the arena was lined with red or black stones. Considering how much blood was shed on the grounds, it made sense that the wall wasn't a color that could be easily stained. Atop the wall were the caves or seating for the spectators.

The Two Gates: Life and Death

When many events started, people would direct their attention to the gates. Animals were often brought up through the floor. People left through two main gates.

- The Porta Triumphalis was for the gladiators who survived, and the name translates as the "Door of Victory." The gladiators also entered through this gate.

- The Porta Libitinaria was for the people who died in the ring. The name of this arch honored the goddess Libitina, who oversaw tombs.

These two archways made it clear who won and who lost. Gladiators did get to enter through the Porta Triumphalis, but they would not all leave through it. Considering how much time, money, and energy went into training gladiators, it wasn't always guaranteed that they would die.

The second gate was not just for the dead, as death was not always guaranteed. When a participant lost, whether they were injured or dead, they exited through this gate. It led down to the gladiator area underground, where they were able to get immediate medical attention.

Once the dead passed through the Porta Libitinaria, they were taken to the Spoliarium. All of their armor and weapons were removed and placed in the Armamentarium for other gladiators to use.

Amenities

The aqueducts that brought water to the Colosseum allowed for mock water battles, but that was not the sole use of water in the facility. One of the most surprising amenities at the Colosseum was the water fountains, as they were similar to the kinds of water fountains you see in stadiums today. Given that the Colosseum was made to seat tens of thousands of people, hundreds of fountains were added to ensure that people had a way of getting water. To ensure there was water, the ancient Romans ran pipes through the walls, and those pipes stored the water that people would drink.

They also had facilities for removing human waste, as well as restrooms. The restrooms were not quite like what we have today (instead of toilet seats, people had to hover over holes), but people were able to use the bathroom, and the waste was then removed through their sewer system.

Perhaps one of the most innovative aspects of the Colosseum was the velarium, a cover that ensured that the spectators were covered from the elements. It protected them from rain and sun when it was needed. The velarium was retractable, so if it was a beautiful day, the spectators were able to enjoy the open sun. When it was raining or when the summer was at its hottest, they would extend the velarium over much of the stadium, shielding the spectators from the elements. The Romans brought in sailors to control the process of retracting and extending the velarium. The material used to make the cover was a unique type of canvas and netting. While it did not extend over the entire inner arena, it did cover roughly two-thirds of it. The people in the arena were generally exposed, but the spectators were mostly comfortable.

Chapter 5 – The Hypogeum and the Connected Schools

Movies and shows have worked to reenact what the spectators saw in the Colosseum, but there was so much occurring under the boards that even ancient Romans didn't know about. It is much easier to see the underground area today, and it is impressive because the masonry is still largely standing. The engineers made an area that was able to withstand everything happening on the wooden panels above, including elephants that were raised up from the underground regions.

The hypogeum is a complex substructure that runs under the arena, taking up the space that used to be the artificial lake. It was entirely different from the arena that the crowd saw. If a person didn't know where they were going, they could easily get lost. That's why today there are tours to walk people through those areas. What's really impressive is that the hypogeum is two stories underground, demonstrating just how complex the ancient Romans' engineering could be.

A view of the arena with a clear view of the hypogeum.[4]

The large labyrinthian layer of the Colosseum has two main corridors, but looking down on it, the corridors look like a thumbprint. When it was designed, the hypogeum was divided into different areas to handle the activities of a wide range of events. For example, there were places for the gladiators, prisoners, animals, and even storage. It is interesting to think about what it would have been like during an event and how people must have felt as the crowds cheered.

It is also important to note that this area was initially not planned or designed to be what it would eventually become. Neither Emperor Vespasian nor Emperor Titus had thought about the logistics of the activities held in the Colosseum. Emperor Domitian decided to use the location under the Colosseum for preparations, which would largely end the water events, as they would damage the structure.

The Tunnels and Devices

Making the hypogeum took a few years, and it required a considerable amount of work to ensure that the people under the stadium would be safe while things were occurring out in the open. They used stone to create eighty different shafts to transport people and animals to the arena. Some of the shafts were also designed to have moving platforms, known as hegmata. The primary purpose of these was to move larger animals and equipment to the surface.

To ensure that they would be able to bring up the large animals and items to the arena, the builders made thirty-six trapdoors. Occasionally, gladiators would be brought up through the trapdoors, but usually, larger items were transported that way to act as a surprise for the spectators. Many of the people who were employed to work in the hot hypogeum were slaves. They worked the machinery and equipment. They also cleaned and tended to the animals.

The tunnels were made to easily move around under the arena, including being able to get out of the Colosseum. Some of the tunnels led to buildings directly outside of the structure. These structures typically housed the participants of the arena and also acted as storage, where items were saved for later use. The Summum Choragium was an outside building that was used for storage.

There were five tunnels leading under the roads and directly into the hypogeum, but only three of them were for the gladiators. Two of the tunnels were used to bring other items and people into the arena.

The Gladiator Areas

Gladiators did not live under the Colosseum. They had their own special tunnels that led from their schools to the tunnels under the arena. When it was time for their fights, they would leave the hypogeum to face off in front of the crowd. To ensure that fighters would be able to properly prepare and fight, a large part of the underground was dedicated to creating spaces for the different needs of the gladiators, even after death. Most of these spaces were in buildings just outside of the stadium, but they were connected by underground tunnels.

The gladiators had a barracks area and a dedicated place for training under the arena, ensuring that they could sleep and practice leading up to their fights. When it was time for them to enter the arena, they went through the Gate of Life, and those who survived their time in the arena would return through it after they were done. These doors lead to the barracks area and other sections that were used by the athletes of the day.

All four main gladiator schools near the Colosseum focused on different types of training, mostly depending on what the gladiators brought into the ring (weapons and armor). For instance, one school focused on how to fight against a very specific type of opponent. Some of the schools used the same tunnels to get to the Colosseum.

Since death was not inevitable, there were medical experts available to start working on gladiators who survived. People who were victorious in a fight could still be injured. Anyone who survived went there to have their injuries treated because (much like today) a lot of money was invested in these very popular athletes. If a gladiator survived the fight, it was important to get him fixed up and ready for his next fight.

Those who died were also brought through the area, but they were put into a morgue.

The Great School

The Ludus Magnus, or the Great School, was where gladiators trained. In the early days, gladiators were mostly slaves and people of lesser stature, but over time, spectators began to hold the successful gladiators in high esteem. Over time, healthy men (and later women, although female fighters were never as popular) volunteered to become gladiators because they wanted some of the prestige that could be won in the arena.

Regardless of their background, gladiators followed the same rules and were mostly trained in the same school. The conditions were different, of course. Enslaved gladiators were not there of their own free will, so measures, such as chaining them, had to be taken to ensure they did not escape. Women fought as gladiators, but it is uncertain if they were trained at the school as the men.

It isn't possible to use the passage from the school to the Colosseum now because a road and sewage system now run through where the tunnel was. It can be visited during a tour, though, as it is just across the street from the impressive structure.

The Bestiarii School

Known as the Ludus Matutinus, this school was for gladiators who specialized in fighting animals instead of people. This school was established at the same time as the hypogeum and had a tunnel that led from the school to the arena. The name means "of the morning" because that was when fights against animals were generally scheduled.

The school was next to the Ludus Magnus. The school had a place to keep the animals while waiting for fights, and they would be moved under the Colosseum prior to the fight.

The Ludus Dacicus Dacian School

Gladiators in this school were usually from Thracian countries, and their weapons of choice were different from the weapons used by more traditional schools. Their favorite sword was a sica, which had a curved blade that was roughly forty to forty-five centimeters (sixteen to eighteen inches) long.

The Ludus Gallicus School

The least common type of gladiator, those who trained in the Ludas Gallicus, wore more armor than the traditional gladiators. They learned Gallic combat, which consisted of powerful attacks. Then, they had to learn to complement their actions with the teachings of Samnite gladiators, who used a short sword.

Gladiators who followed other similarly heavily armored schools joined this school for training and preparation prior to appearing in the Colosseum.

Passaggio di Commodo

In addition to the tunnels used by the gladiators, there was a fifth tunnel that allowed the emperor to enter the arena. This tunnel went from the palace to the arena, giving the emperor a way to avoid being seen coming and going if he wished.

Chapter 6 – Early Uses

Emperor Titus opened the structure to the public around 80 CE with a grand event that lasted one hundred days. The original structure was not fully complete. That would happen about two years later under Emperor Domitian, although by the time of Titus, the structure was completely functional; there was just still work to be done on the upper stories of the structure.

The freestanding structure was like a beacon to people who came to Rome because it was so easily visible from nearly any angle. Most amphitheaters were largely built into hillsides to reduce how much had to be built. By using sturdy arches and columns, the Romans were able to construct something that was solid enough to literally stand on its own. Between the games and the opulence of the structure, word of the Colosseum spread, and it became a significant draw for people well outside of the Roman Empire.

The Colosseum was said to be a gift to the Roman people, and when it opened to one hundred days of games, it was a spectacle that was unlike anything that had come before it.

Emperor Commodus: Failing to Understand the Point of the Colosseum

Following the games, the Flavian Amphitheater became a destination for a wide range of activities. The gladiator matches remained the most famous, but the Romans were able to do a lot more with the large arena.

However, it has been noted that Emperor Commodus actually participated in gladiator fights at the Colosseum.

When Commodus began his reign, he was a co-emperor with Marcus Aurelius, his father, starting around 177 CE. At the time, the young emperor was fifteen years old, something that would prove to be incredibly problematic. Marcus Aurelius failed to acknowledge that his son showed signs of being a poor choice to rule. As one historian, Aelius Lampridius, would eventually write about this early co-emperor situation, "Even from his earliest years he was base and dishonorable, and cruel and lewd, defiled of mouth, moreover, and debauched."

Marcus Aurelius was a beloved emperor, having expanded the empire and understood how to keep the people on his side. He was related to members of the Flavian dynasty, and his family had a prominent place in the empire. As he grew, he learned how to govern. His rise to power is unknown today because he was not the chosen successor to Emperor Hadrian. He was meant to be a joint emperor around his seventeenth birthday, but something happened that meant he did not actually become emperor until he was forty years old. However, he won over a lot of people over those years. He was a great strategist, which was why he was able to help expand the empire, and he was also considered very intelligent. Marcus Aurelius is still known for his philosophy and intellectual pursuits.

Unfortunately, Marcus Aurelius's son did not take after him, and their shared reign did not last long. It is unknown if it would have helped Commodus to learn how to be a better ruler since he was eighteen when his father died, but he certainly was not up to filling his predecessor's shoes. Like Nero and Caligula, Commodus preferred to indulge in all of the benefits of being an emperor without paying enough attention to the people under him. With a large harem and no interest in working, he spent much of his time delegating the important work to other people.

What seemed to interest Commodus the most was gladiator fights. Sometimes, he would attend them, but the emperor was said to have participated in over one hundred events. Not that most of those were particularly fair. The odds were heavily stacked in his favor. It is said that he once killed one hundred bears (which could be an exaggeration) by killing the bears with spears from his seat in the stands. It is also said that he had put men who had lost their feet in the arena. They were forced to dress as snakes and throw sponges at him. Commodus clubbed all of

do the fighting as a part of the battle.

Everyone knew there would be an impressive water battle, so the event attracted thousands of people. It is unclear just how much of what they witnessed was planned and choreographed and how much was the men just improvising and attacking each other. With a large number of attendees and not enough control over a huge crowd, some of the people who came to witness the spectacle were trampled and killed. Ovid would write of the event, "With such a throng, who could not fail to find what caught his fancy?" This indicates that the entertainment went much further than merely spectating, with the event having plenty of debauchery. And this went beyond just drinking, as was highlighted by the number of surrounding brothels and the number of sex workers at the event.

Even though a lot of consideration and care went into making the Colosseum, there was still an element of danger, particularly when it came to filling it with water for the mock battles. Cassius Dio, a Roman historian, would write about the preparation for such a battle at the Colosseum around 235 CE. According to his writings, the mock battle occurred at a time when there was also heavy rain. This account relays that both participants in the battle and members of the audience died during the deluge. If this account is correct, it would explain why the Romans altered the structure, adding the hypogeum to be used for safer events or at least safer events for the spectators.

Chapter 7 – Death in the Colosseum

We largely associate the Colosseum with fighting, whether individuals or mock battles. This was obviously one of the biggest draws to the arena, but fighters were not the only people sent into the Colosseum to die. Rome ruled a large part of Europe, North Africa, and part of the Middle East at its height. The reputation Rome has today was earned through centuries of treating certain populations of their growing empire in ways that would be considered war crimes today.

This chapter looks at the people who were singled out for death in the Colosseum, whether or not that death was inevitable. The amphitheater was open for a little under four hundred years. In that time, historians have estimated that 400,000 people died in the arena. That means that in a single year, one thousand people died to entertain the audience. The gladiators were not the only ones who entered the Colosseum, although they were almost certainly seen as the most valuable people. A lot of those deaths were people whose deaths would be seen as beneficial to the empire.

The Gladiators

It shouldn't come as a surprise that gladiators were the biggest draw. When these athletes were set to fight against other gladiators, the fighters were paired up in a way that is similar to how athletes are assessed for fights today. For example, we have heavyweight boxing matches now.

Gladiators were set to face each other based on their size, skill, school, and record.

In the early days, gladiators were slaves or prisoners. Then, soldiers joined the arena, and eventually, people would voluntarily become fighters. The shift in participants was because of how much respect a gladiator could receive if he was successful in the arena. This raised those in the lower classes if they were successful, especially slaves, as they could be freed. With the chance to gain fame, people were more likely to put their lives on the line.

Regardless of who a gladiator was, they were expected to die without showing any fear of what was to come. They were supposed to entertain the spectators by being honorable, even as they died.

Prisoners and Execution

Public executions were common in Rome, just like they were around the world until the 20th century. However, it wasn't quite like today. Prisoners could be executed in many different ways, and it was often horrific for the people put into the arena for the expressed purpose of dying.

Perhaps the most well-known prisoners to be put into the ring were Christians. There are actually no records of Christians being killed in the Colosseum as martyrs. It's possible that these kinds of killings occurred elsewhere in the empire, but it's not certain that this type of entertainment was brought into the heart of Rome. Early Christians were killed because they were pacifists and refused to worship the Roman gods. They seemed fearless in following their convictions, and by doing so, they helped to spread their religion much farther and faster than nearly any other group. This happened in part because the Romans held bravery in high esteem. It's possible that no Christians were actually killed in the Colosseum, as that would bring a growing religion into the capital and would have shown the spectators just how far the Christians were willing to go for their beliefs.

There are unconfirmed stories of Christians being killed in the amphitheater, with the most famous being St. Ignatius of Antioch. He was said to have been the first Christian put in the Colosseum. He allegedly faced lions. Those reports have him saying, "I am as the grain of the field and must be ground by the teeth of the lions, that I may become fit for His table." Following his execution, over one hundred Christians were shot by archers. It's also possible that this occurred somewhere other than the Colosseum because Christians were killed all across the empire. It is reported that Christians were executed in front of Nero's statue, with the poor people being placed in a brazen bull. These were large bulls that were made of bronze and were hollow inside. People would be placed into the bulls, and then a fire would be set under it. The person inside of it would be burned alive.

Most executions were carried out around noon, allowing people to take a break from their regular activities to watch people be executed. These people had committed major crimes in the empire. Young children were strongly encouraged to watch. This was considered a way of discouraging young people from committing the same crimes.

The heinous crimes that were considered worthy of being shown publicly started as a fairly short list:

- People who deserted from the military
- Rebels against the empire
- Fugitives

It didn't take long for that list of crimes to grow exponentially. Things like crop destruction, theft of goods or cattle, arson, deceiving a customer, being profane in a temple, going back on a promise, perjury, and rape were just a few of the crimes that were added to the list.

The manner of execution also varied based on the citizenship status of the person to be executed. If someone was a Roman citizen, they were decapitated. Since the condemned would not have a long, drawn-out death, it was considered an honorable way to go. This is fairly ironic as the people being executed might have committed some very horrific crimes, so the thought of letting them die honorably was less of a deterrent. For those who weren't Roman citizens, the manner of death was often related to the person's social status and the crime that they committed. People were burned, slain with a sword, crucified, and tortured. Some of the most brutal methods of execution were to have the criminal reenact a myth or historical scene in which the character they portrayed was bound to die. Perhaps the cruelest was throwing the people to a wide range of animals who were just as doomed as the criminal. Naturally, the animals almost always won in those cases, but the animals would eventually be killed during gladiator fights or animal hunts.

Animals Were a Part of the Deadly Entertainment

People were not the only ones to die to entertain the masses. It's been estimated that over one million animals were killed as a part of the spectacles in the Colosseum. Besides the gladiators who were trained to kill them as a part of the regular fights, there were events called venatio, which were animal hunts. The Romans brought animals from all across their sprawling empire just to have them killed in the arena. This was seen as a way of proving just how dominant the empire was since they could bring exotic animals from pretty much anywhere in the known world. Since it was expensive to do this and there was no real financial benefit to the empire, it showed off Rome's wealth too.

Many types of animals were sent into the arena to die, and not all of them were ferocious. Besides elephants, bears, lions, and tigers, the Romans sent rabbits, crocodiles, goats, boars, dogs, deer, and hippopotamuses into the ring. Although there is no solid evidence, it has been reported that so many animals were killed in the arena that a few species went extinct as a result.

Notably missing from the animals who died in the Colosseum were wolves. Romans held wolves in high regard because they saw the animal as religiously significant. This meant that one of the most ferocious animals in the empire, an animal that could fight well as a pack, was not included as entertainment.

Chapter 8 – Medieval Uses of the Iconic Structure

As the Roman Empire crumbled, repairs and renovations on the Colosseum became less frequent. By the Middle Ages, nature and time had ravaged the structure. Humans would further reduce the once-magnificent structure into a literal shell of itself.

Natural Disasters

The first natural disaster to occur at the Colosseum was a fire started by a lightning strike, which caused significant damage in 217 CE. It managed to burn many of the wooden levels on the inside of the structure, and it took over one hundred years to fully repair all of the damage. Final repairs were coupled with renovations, which was why it wasn't done until 320 CE. It is thought that this caused significant structural damage as well, so the interior of the Colosseum wasn't quite the same after the fire was extinguished.

The next major natural disaster that is thought to have affected the amphitheater was the earthquake of 443 CE. This happened toward the end of the Western Roman Empire (historians usually put the fall of Rome around 470 to 500 CE). With the empire in decay, the records were not nearly so well kept, so it is not sure just how much damage the Colosseum suffered because of the earthquake.

There were other fires and earthquakes, but they weren't as significant or costly. The Colosseum ceased to be used for entertainment after

Rome fell, which was when people became the primary means of destroying the historic location. They would begin to plunder it for its valuable materials.

Housing

The rise of Christianity across Europe changed the focus of the power structure. People who were higher up in the religious establishment began to take control over the important structures of the empire, and the Colosseum was a building that offered a lot of potential for use. It came into the hands of friars who lived nearby from 800 to 1349 CE. The place already had a sewage system and other amenities that made it comfortable, and with the tunnels under the arena, it was easy to repurpose the Colosseum into a rental space. The area where animals and gladiators used to wait until they were brought out was changed into living quarters. Walls were built to divide the space into units. The center became a communal area.

The arrangement ended when an earthquake made the residents realize just how dangerous it was to live in this magnificent ruin. With no one having the dedicated time or money to maintain the structure, it was clear to the people who lived in it that the Colosseum wasn't a safe place to live.

The prominent Frangipani family took control of parts of the iconic landmark around 1200 CE. Not much is known about what they did with it, but they did claim the entire structure for a while. It seems likely that they were the ones benefiting from people living in the Colosseum.

Intentional Destruction and Farther Attempts at Use

It isn't clear what happened to the Colosseum over the years once it was clear that the building wasn't a place that had much practical use. However, Rome was the center of the Catholic Church, and Christians wanted to leave their mark around the city and in nearby locations, particularly the Vatican. The Catholic Church firmly believed that the Colosseum was a place where Christians were sacrificed for entertainment. They used the claim that many Christians were martyred in the stadium to claim it for themselves.

The 1349 CE earthquake saw some additional destruction to the structure; it lost some of its concrete and stone, which were critical parts for some of the arches. Large rock and stone chunks lay around the Colosseum, but they did not remain there forever. Christians took these chunks and used them in the construction of several cathedrals, including St. John Lateran and St. Peter. Pieces of the Colosseum were also used in the construction of the Palazzo Venezia and along the Tiber River.

As they built their own structures and less impressive works of architecture, the people who lived around Rome began mining precious materials from the structure. Essentially, they used the Colosseum as a quarry, taking any material that was still usable. By this time, the wood was rotten and not usable, but nearly everything else could be removed, including the marble and more decorative rocks and bricks.

The Catholic Church would try again to use the structure, but this time, the pope was the one who wanted to make the Colosseum something that would be financially beneficial to the area. Pope Sixtus decided that it would be a good place to make wool, so it was transitioned into a wool factory around 1500 CE. After his death, the factory was quickly shut down.

Unfortunately, people would continue to strip parts of the Colosseum away, leaving deep scars from where hinges and bronze clamps had been removed from the walls and doors.

The plundering of the structure was finally declared over by Pope Benedict XIV. He said that it was wrong to do this in the place where so many Christians were martyred. He was the first pope to push for renovations to the structure. People finally began to want to preserve the building that was once the pride of the Roman Empire. It isn't certain when the Catholic Church began to protect the Colosseum (sometime during the 16th and 17th centuries), but it finally started to recognize the importance of preserving one of the greatest engineering feats in human history.

Chapter 9 – The Colosseum in Modern Times

There is no picture of what the Colosseum used to look like. What we recognize today is how it has looked for several hundred years, which is unfortunate because even the ruins are impressive. However, there were events and situations that would continue to threaten the landmark, including two world wars.

During the 19th century, some of the efforts to preserve the structure had evolved from trying to remember the Christians who were supposedly martyred in the Colosseum into an archaeological marvel. People who were interested in understanding more about the structure and the ancient Roman civilization began excavations to understand what their mindset was. Even then, people were aware that the main draw was the gladiator battles, not killing Christians or criminals.

When Italy was reunited in 1870, the Colosseum became a symbol of Italian heritage, not a structure tied to Christianity. It was one of many historical sites that received attention and funding to preserve Italian history. The biggest concern was that the structure was not stable, so they began to fortify some of the weakest parts by adding buttresses. Ironically, the newer buildings around it were torn down to protect the Colosseum and make it easier to conduct necessary repairs.

It doesn't seem that World War I resulted in any problems for the Colosseum, but it was definitely harmed during World War II, mostly because of the dictator Benito Mussolini. He had many of the buildings around the structure demolished, which meant evicting a lot of people around it. This was enforced around the city as a part of a push to highlight ancient artifacts, and it cost thousands of people their homes. This would have a lasting effect on the city since it literally changed the landscape; the historic structures had already been incorporated into daily life. These changes made it so that the Colosseum and many other ancient artifacts were isolated. While this made it easier for tourists, it took away from their historical significance as part of the fabric of the city's life; they were supposed to be more than just shrines to a bygone era.

The dictator and his regime made a lot of changes, leaving their stamp on the capital city. This occurred before World War II began. Once the fighting started, the efforts to change the city to look the way Mussolini wanted ended. He was killed by his people. When the Allies finally took Rome, their tanks moved past the Colosseum. While it did not play a big role in the war, it did have an interesting place in the history of Italy during that time. The Italians quickly surrendered to the Allies, so retaking Italy and Rome was not a significant fight, unlike

Allied troops outside of the Colosseum on leave in Italy in June 1944.[5]

in Germany and Japan. Still, the ancient structure saw the arrival of a major force, and pictures were taken of the event.

It is estimated that only a third of the original structure remained by the time restoration began in earnest during the 20th century. A serious project to start bringing it back to its former glory began during the 1990s. Costing an estimated forty billion lire, the project lasted from 1993 until 2000. Work was done to prop up the weaker parts of the structure, ensuring that no more of the foundation was damaged. While the major project ended at the turn of the century, restoration work continues to this day. Italians strive to preserve this piece of their history.

Chapter 10 – Its Role in Rome and the World Today

In 2007, the Colosseum was named one of the New Seven Wonders of the World. The original seven wonders were constructed in ancient times, but most of them have not survived to the modern day. The Seven Wonders of the Ancient World were the following:

- The Great Pyramid, the largest of the pyramids of Giza, is still standing despite it being over four thousand years old.

- Hanging Gardens of Babylon was thought to have been built as far back as 600 BCE, but nothing of it remains today.

- The Statue of Zeus was said to have been as tall as twelve meters (forty feet), but nothing of it remains today. It was destroyed in an earthquake before the Roman Empire rose to power.

- Temple of Artemis in Ephesus (modern-day Turkey) was destroyed by Herostratus, who reveled in the idea of obliterating the famous temple.

- The Mausoleum of Halicarnassus was built for Maussollos of the Persian Empire. It did not withstand the millennia of earthquakes; only small pieces of the foundation still remain.

- The Colossus of Rhodes was a huge statue of Helios, the personification of the sun. It only stood for about fifty-six years, as earthquakes destroyed everything above the knees (people continued to visit it for nearly another millennia to marvel at what little remained).

- The Pharos of Alexandria, or the Lighthouse of Alexandria, was located near Alexandria, Egypt, from roughly 285 BCE until 1323 CE. It was destroyed by numerous earthquakes by 1500 CE.

With only one remaining ancient wonder and few historians having even a hint of what some of these wonders looked like, it was decided to identify other ancient marvels that have withstood the test of time. This time, the people would look around the world, not just around Europe, North Africa, and the Middle East. The new list started to be compiled in 2000. It had been more than two thousand years since a list had been made, so the Swiss Foundation decided to determine new ancient structures that actually were wonders. These structures were not only impossibly large and detailed, but they were also ingenious creations that could largely withstand the tests of time.

The new list includes the following wonders.

- The Colosseum is nearly two thousand years old and has managed to withstand earthquakes, time, and humans. While it isn't the gorgeous structure that it once was, it is still a marvel that seems to have been built long before it should have been possible.

- The Great Wall of China may not be complete today, but long stretches of it still remain (it is thought to have been over 8,850 kilometers or 5,500 miles). It stretches out longer than the eye can see when standing in the middle.

- Chichén Itzá was a city of the Maya, and much of the ruins of the city remain (even though the people are long gone).

- Petra is an ancient city that was built into the walls of a cavern. Located in Jordan, the city is removed from civilization today, but it was once a popular trade center for the region. It is thought to have been abandoned after several major earthquakes between 360 and 600 CE and was only found again in 1912.

- Machu Picchu is an Incan city that was rediscovered in 1911. There are many theories of what it was meant to be, but there are no real records, as it was abandoned. Located on top of the Andes Mountains, it would have been incredibly isolated from the rest of the Inca population, but it is impressive, even by today's standards. There are tours where people can walk up the Andres over a few days to walk around what remains of the location.

- *Christ the Redeemer*, which is perhaps comparable to the Colossus of Rhodes, is an enormous statue that stretches its arms over Rio de Janeiro, Brazil. It is the youngest wonder on this list; it was built following the end of World War I.

- The Taj Mahal, located in Agra, India, was built to remember Mumtaz Mahal, the wife of Emperor Shah Jahan in the 17th century. It is made of white marble and includes impressive gardens and a reflection pool.

These wonders are awe-inspiring, and almost all of them are sought out by tourists who want to feel the weight of history and the marvel of human ingenuity. The Colosseum is one of the oldest wonders, and it is also one of the most visited because of how steeped in history it is, as well as how innovative its internal workings are.

Conclusion

The Colosseum is famous around the world, and it is recognizable in most places just from a picture of it. Despite being nearly two thousand years old, it remains the largest amphitheater in the world. It offered a place for anyone who wanted to witness the grand events and feel a communal spirit. Food, water, and entry were free, demonstrating the power and wealth of the empire for several hundred years.

Fires and earthquakes continued to damage the majestic structure. Time and people proved to be far more detrimental, though, and it would be over 1,800 years before serious effort and money would be spent to try to restore the impressive building to a more stable state.

Billions of lire have been spent to ensure that no more of the structure is lost, and the building is more stable than it has been in hundreds of years. It is the biggest tourist destination in Rome, and it continues to draw millions of people a year from all over the world. However, the entertainment today is in imagining what it once was like, how people lived, and to marvel at just how advanced the Romans were.

If you enjoyed this book, a review on Amazon would be greatly appreciated because it would mean a lot to hear from you.

To leave a review:

1. Open your camera app.
2. Point your mobile device at the QR code.
3. The review page will appear in your web browser.

Thanks for your support!

Here's another book by Captivating History that you might like

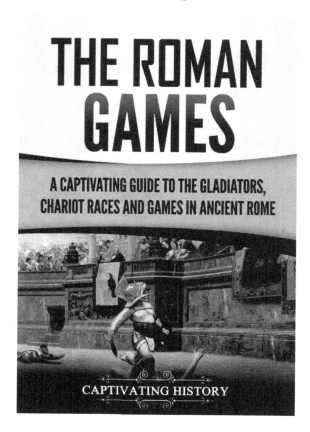

Free Bonus from Captivating History (Available for a Limited time)

Hi History Lovers!

Now you have a chance to join our exclusive history list so you can get your first history ebook for free as well as discounts and a potential to get more history books for free!

Simply visit the link below to join.

Or, Scan the QR code!

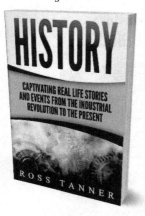

captivatinghistory.com/ebook

Also, make sure to follow us on Facebook, X, and YouTube by searching for Captivating History.

Bibliography

24 Facts About The Colosseum, The Colosseum, May 10, 2024, thecolosseum.org

7 Blood-Soaked Facts about the Colosseum, DarkRome, May 15, 2024, City Wonders Limit, darkrome.com

Afterlife: 18th Century to 20th Century, Piranesi in Rome, May 15, 2024, Omeka, omeka.wellesley.edu

Christian martyrs in the Colosseum, Maria Milani, 2017, Ancient Roman History, mariamilani.com

Colosseum arena, Rome, Italy, The Editors of Encyclopedia Britannica, March 29, 2024, Britannica.com

Colosseum Definition, Mark Cartwright, May 29, 2018, World History Encyclopedia, worldhistory.org

Colosseum, Civitatis, May 10, 2024, civitatis Rome.com

Colosseum, History.com Editors, July 11, 2022, History.com

Colosseum, rome.info, May 10, 2024

Colosseum, The Editors of Encyclopedia Britannica, March 29, 2024, Britannica, britannica.com

Culture in the Ancient Roman Republic, N.S. Gill, September 3, 2019, ThoughtCo, thoughtco.com

Fascist Archeology in Mussolini's Rome, Christopher Siwicki, May 11, 2020, Art&Object, artandobject.com

From Flavian Amphitheater to Colosseum, N.S. Gill, August 5, 2019, ThoughtCo, thoughtco.com

Gladiator Schools in Rome, Linda Alchin, 2017, tribunesandtriumphs.org

History of the Colosseum, The Colosseum, May 10, 2024, thecolosseum.org

History, Facts and Information about Hypogeum, Linda Alchin, 2017, Hypogeum, tribeandtriumphs.org

How Did The Colosseum Get Its Name?, kissformitaly, Sep 29, 2013, kissfarmitaly.com

How the Colosseum Was Built, Farell Evans, July 15,2022, History.com, history.com

Hypogeum of Colosseum, colosseumrometickets, 2018, colosseumrometickets.com

Ludus Magnus Gladiator School in Ancient Rome, Colosseum Rome, 2024, visit-colosseum-rome.com

New Seven Wonders of the World, Amy Tikkanen, "New Seven Wonders of the World," Encyclopedia Britannica, Feb 14, 2018, www.britannica.com

Roman Executions in the Colosseum: The Stories of Laureolus and Androcles, Mauro Poma, May 28, 2017, Ancient Origins, ancinents-origins.net

Romans Once Filled the Colosseum with Water and Staged an Epic Mock Sea Battle, Tao Tao Holmes, January 27, 2016, Atlas Obscura, atlasobscura.com

Secrets of the Colosseum, Tom Muller, January 2011, Smithsonian Magazine, smithsonianmagazine.com

Seven Wonders of the Ancient World, National Geographic, May 15, 2024, education.nationalgeographic.org

The Colosseum, May 13, 2024, thecolosseum.org

The Colosseum, National Geographic Society, October 19, 2023, NationalGraphic.com

The Colosseum: An Engineering Marvel of the Roman Empire, Kashyap Vyas, March 1, 2018, Interesting Engineering, interestingengineering.com

The Colosseum's History, Natasha Sheldon, May 12, 2022, History and Archaeology Online, historyandarchaeology.com

Why is the Colosseum broken?, Rome Tours, May 15, 2024, Sightseeing Tours, romecitytour.it

Image Sources

[1] *https://commons.wikimedia.org/wiki/File:Colosseum-profile-english.png*

[2] *Rc 13, CC BY-SA 3.0 <https://creativecommons.org/licenses/by-sa/3.0>, via Wikimedia Commons; https://commons.wikimedia.org/wiki/File:Colosseum_Ses_Titus_80AD.JPG*

[3] *FeaturedPics, CC BY-SA 4.0 <https://creativecommons.org/licenses/by-sa/4.0>, via Wikimedia Commons; https://commons.wikimedia.org/wiki/File:Colosseo_2020.jpg*

[4] *Charlottev96, CC BY-SA 4.0 <https://creativecommons.org/licenses/by-sa/4.0>, via Wikimedia Commons; https://commons.wikimedia.org/wiki/File:ColosseumInt.jpg*

[5] *https://commons.wikimedia.org/wiki/File:The_British_Army_on_Leave_in_Italy,_June_1944_TR1959.jpg*

Made in the USA
Columbia, SC
07 July 2025

60482784R00033